Handsome Lake: The Life and Legacy of the Iroquois Prophet

By Charles River Editors

Jesse Cornplanter's drawing of Handsome Lake

Introduction

Jesse Cornplanter's drawing of Handsome Lake preaching

Among all the Native American tribes, the Iroquois people are some of the most well documented Native Americans in history. Indigenous to the northeast region of what is now the United States and parts of Canada, they were among some of the earliest contacts Europeans had with the native tribes. And yet they have remained a constant source of mystery.

The name "Iroquois", like many Native American tribal names, is not a name the people knew themselves by, but a word applied to them by their enemies the Huron, who called them "Iroquo" (rattlesnake) as an insult. The French later added the suffix "ois." Moreover, the Iroquois are not even a single tribe but a confederation of several different tribal nations that include the Seneca, Oneida, Onondaga, Mohawk, Cayuga and the Tuscarora, who didn't become part of the union until the early 1700's. The name Haudenosaunee (pronounced "ho-den-oh-SHO-nee") is the name the people use for themselves, which translates as "the People of the Longhouse." They are also commonly known as the Six Nations.

Despite their own cultural differences, the nations that comprised the Iroquois Confederacy established their political dominance across much of America's East Coast and Midwest through conquest, and it is that aspect which has perhaps best endured among Americans in terms of the Iroquois' legacy. European settlers who came into contact with the Mohawks in the Northeast certainly learned to respect their combat skills, to the point that there were literally bounties on the Mohawks' heads, with scalps fetching money for colonists who succeeded in slaying them and carrying away the "battle prize".

In addition to the constant state of conflict between the Iroquois and different nations, including the French and the colonists, the Six Nations are perhaps best known for their political structure, and their influence on American democracy is well documented if not well known by most Americans.

Far from being relics of history, they are living communities who maintain political relationships with United States and Canada, as they have occupied their territories long before international borders were drawn. Their histories have left an indelible mark on the formation of the United States and Canada.

Handsome Lake (1735-1815) lived through the confederacy's most turbulent time. His long life started when the Iroquois were powerful and widely feared and respected by all the tribal peoples in the region, and also by the French and the British. He lived through wars, some victories and some defeats, as well as the disunity and the collapse of traditional ways. Handsome Lake experienced his visions late in his life, at a time when the Six Nations, and his own life, were at their nadir.

The Six Nations

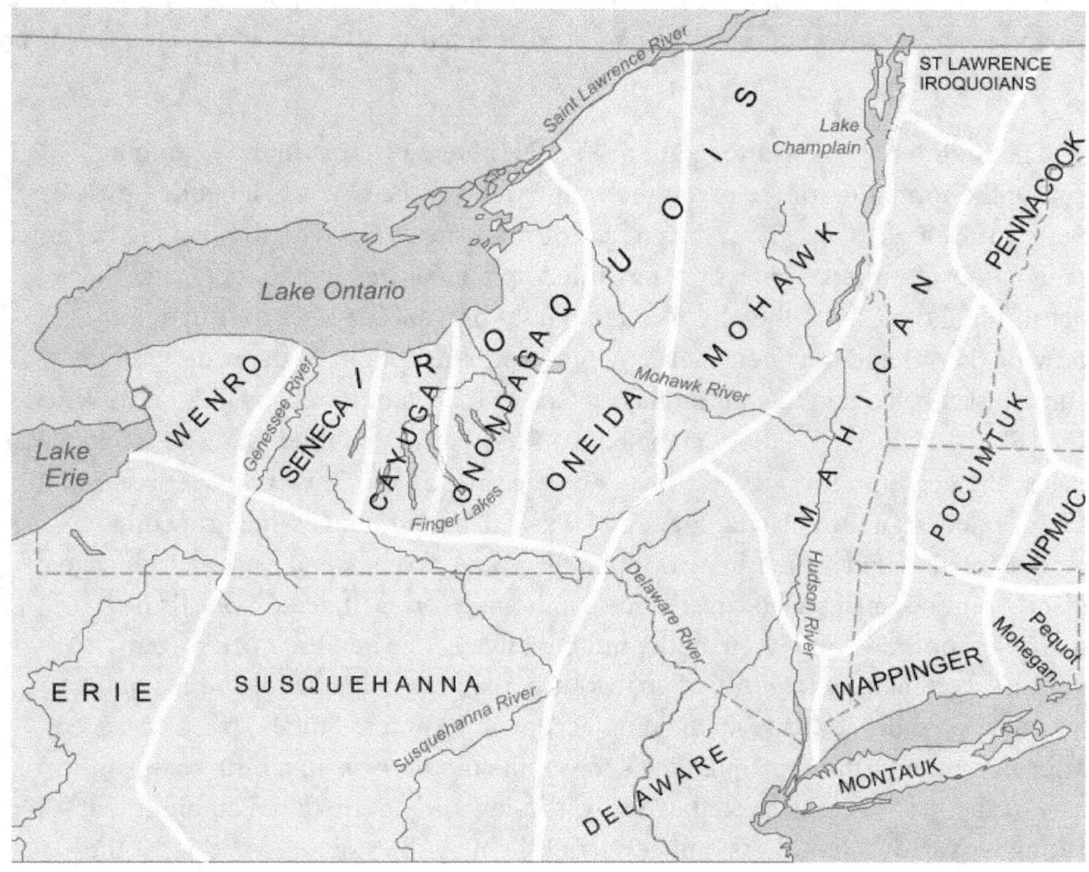

A map of the region

Understanding the enduring importance of Handsome Lake, the Iroquois prophet, requires knowing something about his people and their history. He was from the Seneca tribe, one of the six nations in the Iroquois confederacy. The Iroquois came together in an alliance long before the initial European settlements. They became the most militarily powerful American Indian group during the fierce Beaver Wars in the 1600s, and for almost 150 years managed to play the Dutch against the French, and then the British and French against each other (the Dutch were ousted in 1654).

The origin of the league is shrouded in myth. The traditional story told was that the Creator of the world was concerned with the disunity and fighting among the people, so a prophet was sent, named Deganawidah, who had been born among the Huron people. This man was appointed to seek unity and peace. The story is very complicated, but eventually he converted an evil man, Hiawatha, and together they brought the five peoples together. One of the events concerned in forming the Iroquois confederacy is what historians think was an eclipse that is calculated to have occurred in the Genesee region of New York in 1454, so that has been proposed as a date for the creation of Iroquois unity (P. Wallace "People").

One of the earliest written recordings of the story dates to 1816 by John Norton, who was of Scottish and Cherokee descent and who had been adopted by the Mohawks. This is Norton's rendition of the story:

"The tradition of the Nottowegui or Five Nations says, that in the beginning before the formation of the earth; the country above the sky was inhabited by Superior Beings, over whom the Great Spirit presided. His daughter having become pregnant by an illicit connection, he pulled up a great tree by the roots, and threw her through the Cavity thereby formed; but, to prevent her utter destruction, he previously ordered the Great Turtle, to get from the bottom of the waters, some slime on its back, and to wait on the surface of the water to receive her on it. When she [Sky Woman] had fallen on the back of the Turtle, with the mud she found there, she began to form the earth, and by the time of her delivery had encreased it to the extent of a little island. Her child was a daughter, and as she grew up the earth extended under their hands. When the young woman had arrived at the age of discretion, the Spirits who roved about, in human forms, made proposals of marriage for the young woman: the mother always rejected their offers, until a middle-aged man, of a dignified appearance, his bow in his hand, and his quiver on his back, paid his addresses. On being accepted, he entered the house, and seated himself on the birth of his intended spouse; the mother was in a birth on the other side of the fire. She observed that her son-in-law did not lie down all night; but taking two arrows out of his quiver, he put them by the side of his bride: at the dawn of day, he took them up, and having replaced them in his quiver, he went out.

"After some time, the old woman perceived her daughter to be pregnant, but could not discover where the father had gone, or who he was. At the time of delivery, the twins disputed which way they should go out of the womb; the wicked one said, let us go out of the side; but the other said, not so, lest we kill our mother; then the wicked one pretending to acquiesce, desired his brother to go out first: but as soon as he was delivered, the wicked one, in attempting to go out at her side, caused the death of his mother.

"The twin brothers were nurtured and raised by their Grandmother; the eldest was named Teharonghyawago, or the Holder of Heaven; the youngest was called Tawiskaron, or Flinty rock, from his body being entirely covered with such a substance. They grew up, and with their bows and arrows, amused themselves throughout the island, which encreased in extent, and they were favoured with various animals of Chace. Tawiskaron was the most fortunate hunter, and enjoyed the favour of his Grandmother. Teharonghyawago was not so successful in the Chace, and suffered from their unkindness. When he was a youth, and roaming alone, in melancholy mood, through the island, a human figure, of noble aspect, appearing to him, addressed him thus 'My son, I have seen your distress, and heard your solitary lamentations; you are unhappy in the loss of a mother, in the unkindness of your Grandmother and brother. I now come to comfort you, I am your father, and will be you Protector; therefore take courage, and suffer not your spirit to sink. Take this (giving him an ear of *maize*) plant it, and attend it in the manner, I shall direct; it will yield you a certain support, independent of the Chace, at the same time that it will render more palatable the viands, which you may thereby obtain. I am the Great Turtle which supports the earth, on which you move. Your brother's ill treatment will increase with his years; bear it with patience till the time appointed, before which you shall hear further.'

"After saying this, and directing him how to plant the corn, he disappeared. Teharonghyawago planted the corn, and returned home. When its verdant sprouts began to flourish above the ground, he spent his time in clearing from all growth of grass and weeds, which might smother it or retard its advancement while yet in its tender state, before it had acquired sufficient grandeur to shade the ground. He now discovered that his wicked brother caught the timid deer, the stately elk with branching horns, and all the harmless inhabitants of the Forest; and imprisoned them in an extensive cave, for his own particular; use, depriving mortals from having the benefit of them that was original intended by the Great Spirit. Teharonghyawago discovered the direction the brother took in conducting these animals captive to the Cave; but never could trace him quite to the spot, as he eluded his sight with more than common dexterity!

"Teharonghyawago endeavoured to conceal himself on the path that led to the cave, so that he might follow him imperceptibly; but he found impossible to hide himself from the penetrating Tawiskaron. At length it observed, that altho' his brother saw, with extraordinary acuteness, every surrounding object, yet he never raised his eyes to look above: Teharonghyawago then climbed a lofty tree, which grew near to where he thought the place of confinement was situated: in the meantime, his brother passed, searching with his eyes the thickest recesses of the Forest, but never casting a glance above. He then saw his brother take a straight course, and when he was out of sight, Teharonghyawago descended, and came to the Cave, a short time after he had deposited his charge; and finding there an innumerable number of animals confined, he set them free, and returned home.

"It was not long before Tawiskaron, visiting the Cave, discovered that all his captives, which he had taken so much pains to deprive of their liberty, had been liberated: he knew this to be an act of his brother, but dissembling his anger, he meditated revenge, at some future period.

"Teharonghyawago laboured to people the earth with inhabitants, and to found Villages in happy situations, extending the comforts of men. Tawiskaron was equally active in destroying the works his brother had done; and in accumulating every evil in his power on the heads of ill fated mortals. Teharonghyawago saw, with regret, his brother persevere in every wickedness; but waited with patience the result of what his father had told him.

"At one time, being in conversation with his brother, Tawiskaron said 'Brother, what do you think there is on earth, with which you might be killed?' Teharonghyawago replied, 'I know of nothing that could affect my life, unless it be the foam of the billows of the Lake or the downy topped reed.' 'What do you think would take your life? ' Tawiskaron answered, 'Nothing except horn or flint.' Here their discourse ended.

"Teharonghyawago returning from hunting, heard a voice singing a plaintive air: he listened and heard it name his Mother, who was killed by Tawiskaron; he immediately hastened towards the spot from whence the voice proceeded, crying, 'Who is that, who dares to name my deceased mother in my hearing?' When he came there, he saw the track of a fawn, which he pursued, without overtaking it, till the autumn, when it dropped its first horns; these he took up, and fixed upon the forked branches of a tree.

"He continued the pursuit seven years; and every autumn, when its horns fell, he picked them up, and placed them as he had done the first. At last, he overtook the deer, now grown to be a stately buck: it begged its life, and said, 'Spare me, and I will give you information that may be great service to you.' When he had promised it its life, it spoke as follows, 'It was to give you the necessary information that I have been subjected to your pursuit, and that which I shall now tell you was the intended reward of your perseverance and clemency. Your brother, in coming into the world, caused the death of your Mother; if he was then wicked in his infancy, his malice has grown with his stature; he now premeditates evil against you; be therefore on your guard: as soon as he assaults you, exert yourself, and you will overcome him.'

"He returned home; and not long after this adventure, was attacked by his brother. They fought; the one made use of the horn and flint stone which he had provided: the other sought for froth and the reed, which made little impression on the body of Teharonghyawago. They fought a long time, over the whole of the island, until at last Tawiskaron fell under the conquering hand of his brother. According to the varied tones of their voices in the different places through which they passed during the contest, the people, who afterwards sprung up there, spoke different languages."[1]

Each of the league's initial five member peoples retained independence, each managing its own affairs, giving up only the freedom to make war without the sanction of what might be described as a federal council. The center of the alliance was Onondaga, where councils met yearly, and still do. They spoke dialects of the same basic language, which was not written down. Traditions were transmitted orally, often using woven belts of shells, called wampum, as mnemonic devices to assist a reciter's memory. The five peoples shared the same general kinds of traditions, such as matrilocality and depending on the agricultural "three sisters," corn, squash and beans (deMott).

The easternmost Iroquois, the Mohawks, were designated as the "keepers of the eastern door," and the westernmost Seneca, "keepers of the western door." The Cayuga, Mohawks and Seneca were the "elder brothers." The Oneida in the middle were "keepers of the central council fire." The league would meet periodically to consider matters of peace and war, and to participate in the rituals that knit the allied peoples together (P. Wallace 15).

Iroquois depiction of Adodarhoh two Mohawk chieftains

The Iroquois were, and still are, known as the "Haudenosaunee," meaning simply "the Longhouse people," after the long houses that the peoples traditionally lived in. It has also been

---

[1] Source: Carl F. Klinck and James J. Talman, eds., *The Journal of Major John Norton, 1816* (Toronto: Champlain Society, 1970), 88–91.

called the League of the Iroquois, the Five Nations, and the Iroquois Confederacy. After some Tuscarora refugees joined the league in 1726, the alliance became known as the Six Nations. The peoples commonly refer to the Six Nations as the Haudenosaunee, although each prefers its own specific name in discussing its own traditions.

A traditional Iroquois longhouse

The Six Nations managed to maintain their independence and control over their homeland in what is now New York, despite being sandwiched between two powerful colonial empires. The Iroquois were ultimately shattered by war during the American Revolution and taking sides in the war broke the Iroquois unity.

Following the demise of New France in 1763 and following the Revolution a few years later, the proud Six Nations were reduced to being wards of the British or Americans. By the 1790s, most of their once extensive lands had been lost and were still being lost. A flood of settlers was reducing them to a small minority in their historical homeland. Alcohol was fueling violence and the dissolution of clans and family structure.

The Seneca religious tradition saw the human world as lodged between the sky world and the underworld, in a state of suspension between good and evil. The key to a good and righteous life was living in harmony with the spirit forces, to observe the rites and to respect creation. Shamans, often called "medicine men," thought that illness often resulted from some imbalance between an individual and the spirit forces around them. It was believed that some people were evil, and witches were suspected, feared and despised. Handsome Lake was a medicine man, as well as a chief (St. John "Iroquois").

The "medicine men" could deal with illness by using their knowledge of hundreds of medicinal plants. They could use plant medicines to combat and even cure many ailments. Shamans tried to understand if there was witchcraft involved in an illness, and rituals that led to visions helped them diagnose if a sickness or injury was related to some glitch with the spirit world. They might diagnose that a particular ritual needed to be performed. They would ordinarily be presented with gifts as a kind of payment.

The Iroquois peoples had one of the most complex social structures of any North American Indian groups. Five different peoples came together to form an alliance at some unknown point in the past, which may have been anywhere from the 1100s to the 1400s. From roughly the Hudson River Valley in the east, the peoples in order were the Mohawk, Oneida, Onondaga, Cayuga and Seneca. The Seneca were by a considerable margin the most numerous. Originally, the Iroquois lived in what is now New York, occupying most of the state, and from the Hudson to Lake Erie, and from Lake Ontario to the northwest of what is now Pennsylvania (St. John "Iroquois").

They acquired the name "People of the Longhouse" because the dwellings of all five tribes were large and up to a hundred feet long, literally long houses, made from timber and bark. A number of families lived in each longhouse, with fires in the middle and sleeping and storage areas along the sides. Families had rooms along the sides of the longhouse, separated by partitions made of bark, deerskins or other materials. They often lived in semi-permanent palisaded villages, each composed of a number of the longhouses. The villages needed to be relocated every few years because of reduced fertility of the soil caused by agriculture (P. Wallace "People").

The Iroquois were matrilineal; family descent was reckoned in the female line, and a man was concerned with his sisters' children, not so much his own. Women had a strong voice in tribal councils, and actually chose and advised chiefs. Women owned and managed the land, the lodge and its equipment, and most utensils, and did most of the agricultural activity. Marriages were usually arranged by the mothers of the bride and groom. Councils of women, clan mothers, elected the fifty "sachems," civil chiefs, although not the war chiefs. Some of these traditions relating to clan membership and family descent still remain.

In the absence of a male chief, a woman of rank sometimes became a kind of regent. Some families were traditionally influential, and women from these families had even more status. Women could also recall a sachem who was considered not to be fulfilling his duty properly. Women planted crops, using a hoe and a digging stick, and foraged for foods such as berries and nuts. The men hunted and fished, built canoes, built the lodges, participated in trading and councils, and made war. Women usually decided the fate of prisoners, whether they would be killed or adopted (P. Wallace "People").

Following the French settlement in Canada in 1608, the Iroquois were endangered by attack from enemies who obtained guns through their trade in beaver pelts with New France. The

Iroquois were able to trade for guns with the Dutch post at Albany in the Hudson Valley after its founding in 1614, again trading in beaver pelts, which they sometimes obtained by war and raiding.

Traditional warfare had been small scale. A war party that suffered casualties was regarded as a failure. The introduction of guns early in the 1600s made war among the tribes more deadly and increased its scale. Obtaining beaver pelts to be able to buy guns meant that other tribes had to obtain guns to defend themselves and protect their resources, in a sort of spiral of violence.

Beaver pelts had great value in Europe. The pelts were processed to get rid of the outer hairs so the shorter hair could be used in manufacturing hats. This shorter hair was what kept the animals warm in the cold northern winters, and also produced superb felt for making hats. The long-term fashion in France and the rest of Europe for beaver hats kept the trade in beaver pelts going strong for generations. Beaver from Russia and northern Europe had been long since depleted.

The animals became more and more scarce in the initially exploited areas, so the trade inevitably kept moving ever more to the west and northwest, drawing more and more Indian peoples into the trade. The beaver trade was a disruptive force in almost all the tribes that participated. With beaver pelts to trade, they could acquire far more efficient tools, steel knives and hatchets, iron pots, and guns. Hunting shifted from subsistence to commodity production. There was nothing else that offered comparable profit in New France. Beaver pelts are what drew the French traders out from the initial settlements at Quebec and Montreal to the Great Lakes and beyond.

There was a huge amount of violence and dislocation during the "Beaver Wars," which lasted the better part of a century, from the early 1600s through 1703, when the French managed to broker a peace. The valuable beaver pelts were the currency with which native peoples acquired guns. Guns in the hands of enemies are what, at first, threatened the Iroquois, and then acquiring guns is what enabled the Iroquois to expand as they won war after war. Alcohol was also involved in the trade, to which many Indians found themselves addicted.

An 18th century depiction of the Iroquois engaging in trade with Europeans

An unexpected event profoundly affected all the tribal peoples in the Northeast and Great Lakes region. In 1639, a smallpox epidemic broke out and ran until about 1641. It is estimated to have killed about 10,000 Iroquois, probably half the population of the Five Tribes. The relatively low population density and geographical isolation had protected the people from epidemics that had devastated other areas of the Americas before then. Smallpox was probably carried into the interior by French traders, or by Indian trading groups returning home from the Dutch or French trading posts.

Outbreaks of disease plagued the Iroquois. One or another of the tribes suffered significant mortality from disease outbreaks in 1647, 1656-57, 1661-63, 1668, 1673 and 1676 (Richter 537).

This heavy depopulation shook traditional societies to the core. A series of conflicts erupted, called the "Mourning Wars," which overlapped with the Beaver Wars. The Iroquois lost many warriors in these wars and to epidemics. They remedied their losses by a process of adoption, making war to obtain captives to replace their losses.

Making war in order to obtain captives for adoption was an Iroquois tradition but had been usually in the form of small war parties intent on capturing only a few people. Such raids were often at the behest of clan women who had suffered a loss. Small raids were also conducted by young men intent on making a name for themselves, because success in war greatly enhanced a man's status, and made him more likely to receive honors, such as being appointed a sachem (Richter 528).

The increased mortality from disease and from war increased the importance and intensity of mourning wars. Iroquois population was reduced to about 8,500 by the late 1600s, and the number of warriors dropped accordingly, making defense difficult. French counterraids periodically devastated some of the Iroquois. Raids and counterraids during the long wars between the French and the British eroded Iroquois strength (Richter 546, 551).

The Iroquois had repeatedly raided New France, getting to the outskirts of Montreal. The French counterraids involved as many as 2,000 French regulars, Canadian militia and allied Indians. In 1687, some 30 Iroquois captives were sent to France to become galley slaves (Richter 546).

Over time, thousands of prisoners were taken back to Iroquois. Clan mothers decided their fate. Women might become slaves, or wives, and work in the fields. Adult male captives might be made into slaves or executed. A large number were adopted, often assuming the identity of a killed Iroquois warrior. The adoptee would assume the social role and name of the deceased and become a full member of the tribe. Captives who were accepted replaced sons, fathers, brothers and husbands. Children might be raised as Iroquois. These adoptions strengthened the Six Nations.

Apparently, it was rare for such an adoptee to try to return to his previous identity, because of the infamy of having been captured. Sometimes prisoners were killed and ritually boiled and eaten. This seems macabre to modern sensibilities, but it was seen by the Iroquois in the 1600s as a way of consuming the courage and spiritual power of the dead warrior, enhancing the spiritual power and courage of the participants (Hamalainen 21-22).

The Iroquois also sometimes welcomed refugee tribes, granting them some territory in the Iroquois lands, most notably the Tuscarora refugees, who had been shattered in wars in the Carolinas. The Tuscarora were granted equality with the existing five members of the league, perhaps because they spoke a language not too much different than the Iroquois dialects, and they substantially reinforced the league. The five tribal members became the Six Nations. There was ample room for them in the Iroquois lands in New York. The Tuscarora remain one of the Six Nations. A few other groups found refuge but were not given league membership (St. John 11-12).

A prisoner slated for execution might be allowed to live for several days, and even give a death feast at which he could recite his victories at war. Torture during the execution allowed the captive to demonstrate his courage and strength (Richter 533-34).

Over time, the portion of Iroquois whose origins were captives and adoption became a large element of the total population. French missionaries in the 1690s estimated that two thirds or more of the people in some villages were adopted. How well the process of assimilating them to the Iroquois way worked is not known (Richter 591).

The Beaver Wars resulted in the Iroquois becoming the dominant people over a huge region. The alliance was ruthless in dealing with enemies. They nearly destroyed the Huron in 1648-49, defeated and scattered the Neutrals and the Erie in 1654, and the Susquehannock in 1675. Iroquois raids into the Ohio country turned the Shawnee into a diaspora people, scattering them over the Southeast. Iroquois raided as far west as Illinois in the 1650s and raided the Cherokee and Choctaws in the Southeast during the 1670s.

A number of tribes agreed to recognize Iroquois supremacy. By the end of the 1600s, the league was dominant from the Hudson River to the Illinois country and from southern Canada to the Carolinas. Their dominance lasted for many years, and they remained strong well into the 1700s (St. John 10-11).

Another result of the wars and epidemics was the depopulation of most of the region from the Ohio River to the upper Great Lakes. Over a generation, thousands perished in the wars, thousands were taken prisoner, and many peoples fled west, reconstituting themselves in the land west of Lake Michigan and south of Lake Superior. They had iron weapons and they had guns, so they were able to push many of the tribal peoples already there to the west, including the people known as the Lakota Sioux, who a century later would themselves become a powerful people who adopted the Plains life of horses and pursuing the buffalo (Hamalainen 22).

The Iroquois tried to be neutral in the French and Indian War of 1755-63. They had for generations been able to play the French and British off against each other. However, when France was ousted from virtually all of North America following their defeat in 1763, the strategic position of the Iroquois between two colonial empires was altered and their position quickly began to deteriorate (P. Wallace 26-27).

In 1768, the Iroquois and British agents met at Fort Stanwix in New York, and negotiated the Treaty of Fort Stanwix, in which they agreed to sell their rights to all the land south of the Ohio River and west of the Appalachian Mountains. By then, Iroquois dominance over that area had greatly diminished (Izzo 112).

The Ft. Stanwix cession represents a considerable reduction of Iroquois power over the land they once dominated. In 1768, the Iroquois were still a fairly powerful force, but that would soon be finished forever. There was also a later treaty with the independent Americans with the same name, that also resulted in the cession of more Iroquois lands. As a chief, Handsome Lake probably was involved in this history, but little is known of him in this era.

When the American Revolution began, the Six Nations initially tried to be neutral. However, the British Indian agent Joseph Brant, himself a powerful Mohawk leader, led most of the Iroquois into alliance with the British. Brant's sister had married the highly influential British agent Sir William Johnson, who was Superintendent of Indians in the northern part of the British American colonies. Through that connection, Brant had an excellent education, and was highly thought of by the British.

Brant visited Britain when the war started. He was promised that alliance with the British would be advantageous in land and support following the war. He calculated that the British would suppress the rebellion and reward their Indian allies. The Iroquois still had several thousand warriors, and their support was important.

A 1776 portrait of Brant by painter George Romney

The British also realized that gifts and presents to the Indian peoples were important. The French had regularly budgeted for a large volume of such subsidies as a cost of their alliance system and maintaining the beaver trade. The British had largely abandoned the system after ousting the French, and in 1775 in their Great Lakes posts at Detroit, Michilimackinac and Niagara had provided 500 pounds sterling worth of gifts. After reassessing the value of Indian allies, the British increased the subsidy to 100,000 pounds worth of goods by 1781.

The gift exchange system was partly symbolic of alliance, but also provided the tribes with knives, cooking gear, guns and gunpowder, cloth, sometimes clothing and other useful or decorative things. Most Indians thought that the British would win, and that the British were more likely to provide goods and less likely to want Indian lands (Taylor 254).

Brant led the Mohawk, Seneca, Cayuga and Onondaga to support the British. The Oneida and some of the Tuscarora fought with the Americans. This split the unity of the Six Nations, and after the war ended, many of the Iroquois who had supported the British moved to what is now Ontario in Canada, fearing vengeful Americans. This was not a matter of complete support, because individual Onondaga or Mohawk supported the Americans, and some Oneida sided with the British (P. Wallace 27).

As a Seneca chief, Handsome Lake would have been involved in these debates, and as a warrior. His participation in the fighting is little known. The frontier was sparsely settled, with homesteads and settlements widely scattered and vulnerable to raids. American settlers had begun to flow over the Appalachians, into Kentucky and down the Ohio before the Revolution. Indian allies were the most effective way of interrupting the settlement process, both in the Revolution and the War of 1812 a generation later. Fighting on the frontier was often brutal and savage on both sides. It also increased the hatred of many Americans for all Indians, not just the enemy tribes.

The Iroquois who had sided with Britain during the American Revolution, four of the Six Nations, paid a very heavy price for their choice. In the late summer of 1779, a large American expedition under Generals John Sullivan and James Clinton ravaged most of the Senecan and Cayuga homeland. They led thousands of Continental troops and some militia on an extended raid that burned more than 40 Iroquois towns and villages and destroyed a large amount of stored corn and other food. It was intended as a scorched earth campaign, and it succeeded. More than 5,000 Indians took refuge at British Ft. Niagara, placing a large strain on British resources for conducting the war (NPS "Clinton").

The Revolution was, to an extent, a civil war among the Six Nations. In 1780, Loyalists and British Iroquois raided the Oneida and burned their villages. Some of the Oneida fled to the British post at Niagara, and most of the rest fled to American protection at Schenectady, New York. American settlements in the Mohawk Valley were vulnerable without the Oneida screen and most of the settlements were destroyed, leaving hundreds of widows and 2,000 orphans. The Iroquois refugees on both sides faced cold, neglect, disease and malnutrition (Taylor 257-57).

The 1779 Sullivan campaign seriously damaged the Iroquois war-making potential. However, raids along the western frontier of New York, Pennsylvania and Virginia continued with brutal fighting, until the end of the Revolution. The Iroquois were not the only tribes involved. The toll is unknowable, perhaps several thousands, and it resulted in pushing back the frontier and destroying dozens of settlements.

The British strategy from late in the Revolution was apparently to support the Indian peoples as a screen helping to protect Canada from the flood of American settlers. The British hoped to retain the Great Lakes country and alliance with the Indians was seen as helping that claim. Indian resistance to settlement in what is now Ohio and Indiana was fierce and successful into the 1790s, with the British quietly supplying the tribes with guns and other materials. The Six Nations were not involved in that fighting.

The Iroquois are today scattered on reservations in New York, Ontario, Wisconsin and Oklahoma, but once were centered in New York state, occupying most of it. They were once the most powerful tribe in North America, dominating from the Hudson Valley west to Illinois and from Lake Ontario down nearly to the Carolinas and Tennessee. The only other comparable Native American powers were also alliances, the formidable Comanche centered on the Texas panhandle, and the famous Lakota on the Northern Great Plains. Today, they still retain a sense of unity despite the physical dislocation.

Handsome Lake the Man

Handsome Lake was born into the Seneca Wolf Clan, but was later adopted into the Turtle Clan, and he became a sachem of the Turtle Clan.

Handsome Lake grew up in the traditional Seneca religious traditions and spent most of his life observing them. These Seneca traditions, similar to the other Iroquois peoples, included the belief that the world was created by a pair of cosmic twins, one of whom was evil, the other good. The sky world was above the earthly plane, and was characterized by order, the good, light and life. The underworld below was characterized by chaos, evil, darkness and death, represented in the human world by witches and disrespect for the spirits.

"Handsome Lake" is the English translation of *Ganioda'yo*, Handsome Lake's Seneca name. He is called variously Handsome Lake, the Seneca Prophet, and the Iroquois Prophet. Among the Six Nations itself, his Iroquois name is used, with slight variants among the tribes.

Handsome Lake was born in 1735 and at first named Hadawa'ko, translated as "Shaky Snow." Little is known of his early years. His mother, Gahonneh, had a son by a Dutch trader, his younger half-brother Cornplanter. The prophet is also called *Ganiodaio*, a variant spelling and pronunciation, which simply meant Handsome Lake. His name is also sometimes spelled Skanadariyo, but the meaning is the same. The name was also an honorific title as much as a name. His family was historically important, and he was one of 50 chiefs who made up the central council of the Iroquois confederacy (A. Wallace "Handsome" 152).

Not a lot is known of his youth or when he came of age. He is thought to have participated in several raiding war parties, as would be expected of a Seneca warrior. In 1765, Handsome Lake was part of a war party that raided the Choctaw and Cherokee, long-distance raids that would have taken many weeks and covered hundreds of miles.

In 1778, he was part of a warrior council that met with the British. Many at the council argued that the Revolution was a white man's quarrel, and that the Iroquois should remain neutral because it did not concern them. However, the Seneca decided to join with the British, and, in 1778, Handsome Lake apparently joined war parties attacking a fort and apparently also participated in raiding settlements in the Wyoming Valley region in Pennsylvania. The Wyoming attack devastated a frontier region and resulted in hundreds of settler deaths (Native roots).

The Seneca to which Handsome Lake belonged to were the westernmost of the Iroquois, and they probably had the largest number of people ever since the alliance had begun. They observed the Seneca versions of general Iroquois traditions. The alliance helped the peoples endure military defeat and the Seneca, as well as the other tribes in the alliance, managed to continue to exist in their historical homeland and many remain there to this day. Most other Indian peoples east of the Mississippi were voluntarily or forcibly removed west. Some of the Iroquois resistance was enabled by the message of Handsome Lake.

Handsome Lake came from an important Seneca family, several of whom lived exceptionally long lives. His half-brother, the chief Cornplanter, lived well into his 80s (c1750-1836), and his nephew Red Jacket lived to be 80 (c1750-1830). The prophet himself lived to be 80, despite his long period of addiction to alcohol prior to his visions at age 64.

The 1783 agreements that ended the Revolution did not much consider Britain's Indian allies, so, in effect they were left to the mercy of the Americans. For a time, the Iroquois managed to retain a substantial amount of land, although they lost most of it within a generation. The American raids into Iroquois lands had exposed thousands of American soldiers to the rich agricultural potential of that land, and many came back as settlers.

In 1797, in the Treaty of Big Tree, the Seneca were pressured to sell most of their historic homeland in New York. They did so, turning over 3.5 million acres for deferred payment and some other rights such as hunting and fishing. They sold more of their remaining lands in 1826 and 1835. Some of the deals resulted in controversy over the legitimacy. Once the Six Nations had dictated the terms of treaties, but now they were reduced to fragmented peoples scattered over reservations.

The new reality of the Six Nations was a population nearly swamped by waves of many thousands of settlers, the loss of most of their historic lands, and the necessity to adapt to farming. Alcohol was then the way many Iroquois tried to cope with change. Handsome Lake's very strong opposition to alcohol fit well with Christian missionaries also emphasizing banning drinking. This was Handsome Lake's reality, too.

Cornplanter managed to negotiate with the Americans in such a way that he was granted in perpetuity some lands in the northwest part of Pennsylvania, which came to be called the Allegheny Seneca, because the land was on the river of that name. The land was granted by the state of Pennsylvania, not by the federal government, so it was technically his private property. His close association with the Quakers helped preserve the land, because they helped prevent him from being swindled out of it. He had lost other land in New York to shady manipulation by land agents.

The settlement headed by Cornplanter was called Burnt House. It was for years Handsome Lake's home and refuge, and the scene of his prolonged pitiable condition before he received his visions. It was also his home during the first years of his new religion. About 400 people lived there. It's not clear when Handsome Lake first began abusing alcohol, but by the 1790s he was ineffective as a chief, an aging invalid who was dependent on his relatives for food and shelter.

Before he emerged as a prophet, Handsome Lake was a shaman and a sachem, that is, a "medicine man" and one of the Seneca chiefs. Shamans were concerned with health and the spirit world, assuming sickness was sometimes a consequence of some kind of malevolent magic, or some problem in a patient's life that put them out of kilter with the spirits. Shamans traditionally fasted, danced, interpreted dreams and sometimes experienced trances in which they received messages from the spirit world. They would have early in their training have experienced a dream or vision that would reveal their personal guardian spirit (St. John "Iroquois").

19th century depiction of an Iroquois dancer

Although he was a chief, his increasing use of alcohol made him essentially an invalid, living on the charity of his half-brother. Cornplanter had two cabins, and one was also used for guests. It's not clear which one Handsome Lake lived in. On June 15th, 1799, he had an intense vision, and described it to the people. Two Quaker missionaries also lived for a time in Cornplanter's cabins, so they would have known Handsome Lake and he would have known them. Not long after the vision, he dictated some details about it to Henry Simmons, one of the missionaries (A. Wallace "Handsome" 154-55).

The Oneida Nation describes how *Shakoyatisu*, the Creator, sent four messengers to Handsome Lake. He was sick, and his family thought he was going to die. He lay unconscious for, it is said, four days and had visions, and heard messages from the four messengers. Among the things Handsome Lake was told was that he was not to see himself as anything special because all are created equal, and that he was simply chosen to spread the word. The messages included that the people should continue to do the Great Feather Dance because it would lift the peoples' spirits, and that they should drink strawberry juice (Williams).

Handsome Lake told his people that the Creator abhors alcohol. Alcohol was meant as medicine for the white man, he said, but it has been abused and it violates the will of the Creator, who blew life into all. The sum of Handsome Lake's messages has come to be called *Kaliwihyo* in the Oneida language, which is commonly called The Code of Handsome Lake in English. There are several versions of the prophet's initial visions.

Handsome Lake (1735-1815) did not experience his visions until he was an old man, in 1799. His visions and preaching were passed down orally, with variant versions being written down, but an authoritative version was only written down a century later. There are some brief descriptions written by Quaker observers.

During his long life, the Iroquois went from being a powerful tribal confederacy to a society struggling to survive. The nations survived bitter defeat in the American Revolution, split between supporters of the Americans and supporters of the British, being scattered from Pennsylvania to Ontario, the onset of poverty and the massive loss of land. The prophet was by no means the only man who sought escape in alcohol (St. John 1-2).

Handsome Lake the Prophet

Handsome Lake was a shaman and belonged to an important family. He had become a drunk and lived on the charity of his family. These are important elements in his story. He had important advantages of birth and status, but his life had become a shambles because of his constant drunkenness. He wrecked his health and, the story goes, after several days of illness, he was near death, and then he experienced something that would change his life and change the lives of the Iroquois peoples.

On June 15, 1799, he got up from his presumed death bed, stumbled out of the house and fell to the ground. His daughter Yewenot and her husband Hatgwiyot found him unconscious and carried him back inside to his bed. He was in some kind of near catatonic state, his family was sure he was dying, and began preparing for the death ritual. The stories vary a bit. One story has it that they found a warm spot on his chest and knew he was still clinging to life.

A variant of the story is that Handsome Lake was actually dead, and his daughter dressed him is his best clothes, befitting a chief, and sent messengers to the relatives and clan that he was dead. They came and sat around, mourning the dead man and, after several hours, he awoke, coming back from the land of the dead (Fadden 346).

During his catatonic state, the messengers appeared to Handsome Lake and told him of both a heaven and a hell, of the joy for the faithful and the punishments for sinners. He described the particulars of punishment for some kinds of sin, such as people guilty of gambling being punished with white hot cards that burned the flesh off their hands. Gambling was another common activity with negative consequences for the Seneca, which may account for Handsome Lake's dwelling in the details. The duality of heaven and hell may have come from Christian influence on the prophet (Tucker 191).

When he came back to consciousness, the family was amazed. Handsome Lake sat up and began to describe how three messengers had spoken to him and given him commands from the Creator. He told of the assurance the Creator was concerned with the people. He said that the message from the Creator was summed up in five words - whiskey, witchcraft, love, magic and abortion, all these being things the Creator despised (Native Roots).

He described the three messengers from the Creator that spoke to him during his vision as middle-aged men wearing old time Indian style fine clothes, and of serious bearing. The usual term for them is "messengers," but they have also been described as "angels." The Seneca took visions very seriously, and he would have been listened to carefully. His account of the vision would have been discussed thoroughly by the community, not just the family (Izzo 117).

Handsome Lake experienced an intense second trance several weeks after his first, which lasted seven hours. This vision has been described as the "sky journey," in which he met George Washington and Jesus. Washington was the only white man allowed near Heaven because he respected the Iroquois, said Handsome Lake. Jesus told Handsome Lake how he was sent by the Creator as a prophet to the white people and that they had rejected his message and killed him.

In the sky journey, he was given glimpses of heaven and hell. A moral code was revealed to him that included a ban on alcohol, a prohibition of witchcraft, and bans on promiscuity, quarreling and gambling. He saw the punishments that sinners would experience if they did not reform, and he felt assured that the righteous dead were with the Creator (Izzo 123).

His third intense vision came on February 5th, 1800. In this vision, the Creator told him that the people were to retain four traditional ceremonies as especially important to their happiness. The Great Feather Dance was to honor children and life. The Drum Dance was to honor the spirit beings. The Men's Chant was to honor the Creator, and the Peach Pit Bowl Game and sustenance dance was to amuse the people (Native Roots).

He also announced that there were lesser sins, including unfaithfulness to one's spouse, dancing to the fiddle, gambling at card playing, and reluctance to have children. During his second trance, he described how he was shown two huge spheres suspended in the eastern sky, one red and one yellow. If either were to fall, calamity would result. During his intense vision in 1800, the Creator expressed concern about the loss of Iroquois land. Handsome Lake was instructed to tell the people that they must keep some of the traditional ceremonies, particularly the Midwinter Ceremony.

Handsome Lake's visions and his preaching based on them emphasized the nuclear family rather than living with many others in a long house, although long houses were largely gone by this date. He wished men to become farmers, and this went against Iroquois tradition in which agriculture was women's work. He did not envision farms like the white peoples', who raised crops and sold them; surplus from the Seneca farms was to be shared with the poor and freely given, not sold. His visions did not fit with the tradition of matrilineal descent and other important women's roles, replacing it with a somewhat more patriarchal view (Native Roots).

While his vision included elements common to several other Native American prophets, there was one major difference. Handsome Lake's prophecy did not declare an immediate appearance of the new world, or an apocalyptic end to the world and the demise of white people. The Creator in Handsome Lake's version did not intend to end the white people's existence or return them to where they came from (Izzo 126).

He did say the world might end if the people did not follow the Creator's will, but there was no immediacy and consequently no apocalyptic fervor among converts such as that generated by the Ghost Dance later in the century.

While his code was tough on sinners, Handsome Lake also emphasized confession and repentance. People acknowledging moderate sins could confess privately to him and be forgiven. The messengers had told Handsome Lake that his own sins were forgiven because of the suffering he had been through. They had tried to reach others to deliver their message but were not able to (Izzo 117).

He made four predictions that, when fulfilled, would indicate that the end of the world was at hand. The Iroquois chiefs would begin to argue among themselves and abandon the Great Council. People would abandon the traditional ceremonies and turn to witchcraft. A woman past childbearing age would have a child, and a child would have a baby (Native Roots).

Three messengers were involved in the visions, although he described a fourth, who would later come to visit him when the Creator decided it was time for Handsome Lake to leave the earth, to guide and accompany the prophet on that last trip.

There were witnesses to some of Handsome Lake's visions and early preaching who supplied valuable accounts. Several Quaker missionaries were resident in or near the Alleghany Seneca at the time of the visions. A Quaker named Halliday Jackson was a missionary there from 1798-1800, one of three Quakers. The Quakers were trusted, whereas other Christian missionaries were not, because the Quakers were not interested in Seneca land, and had considerable respect for the Indians. The missionaries knew Handsome Lake, and were there at the explicit invitation of Cornplanter, the leader of the Allegheny Seneca.

The Quakers were quite important in the Handsome Lake story. Cornplanter spoke English and had spent several months in Philadelphia in the winter of 1790, where he met Quakers and attended Quaker services. He came to trust the Quakers as people who respected Indians and had no desire for Indian lands (Deardorff 84).

Cornplanter invited the Quakers to come to Burnt House and set up a school. It took several years, but the Philadelphia Quakers sent several missionaries. They did more than set up a school. They kept journals that supply most of the details we know about the Allegheny Seneca and Handsome Lake at that time. The Quakers also wanted to help the Seneca transition to a farm economy. In 1800, for example, they set up an experiment, using the plow to plant corn, and having women plant the traditional way with the hoe. The yield of the corn planted using the plow was much larger and convinced the Seneca of the plow's superiority (Deardorff 94).

The Quaker missionary journals provide some useful details. We know that some of the changes usually thought to have come from Handsome Lake's movement actually predated his visions. Cornplanter had forbidden alcohol. The journals also describe confession, which was a part of Handsome Lake's Code. Before that, the Seneca had a ceremony twice a year that involved an examination of all the men, women and children as to whether they had committed any offenses or evil actions. The offender often confessed in public, and the council forgave an offender confessing and promising to do better. Handsome Lake's Code incorporated these elements (Deardorff 93).

The Quaker journals allow something of an assessment of Handsome Lake's program. It's evident that some of his new dispensation was a codification of traditional Seneca elements, with an admixture of Quaker ideas. The fact that some of his code was already rather familiar probably made people find it acceptable.

As did other Quakers, Jackson wrote an account based on his diary, as a sort of report to the Quaker community back in Philadelphia. The account is not long and is written in a highly stylized manner that makes it difficult reading. He does describe Handsome Lake as saying that his vision included talking with three messengers, each carrying a green branch, each a different kind of fruit, and eating the fruit would make the sick Handsome Lake cured (A. Wallace 146-47).

Jackson wrote that "…when they heard these things, they danced exceedingly, and they slew a white dog and did eat the flesh thereof." The reference was to the traditional White Dog ceremony of thanksgiving, when a white dog was ritually killed and eaten as part of a purification ceremony. The Seneca liked their dogs, so sacrificing one was not an everyday occurrence. The ceremony Jackson referred to is an indication that some of the people were receptive to Handsome Lake's story. The ceremony stopped being performed about 1800 (A.

Wallace 146-47).

Later, in 1830, Jackson wrote *Civilizations of the Indian Nations*, which mentioned Handsome Lake. The publication is one of several accounts by people who talked with or knew the prophet. This account appears to have been based on the diary he kept when he was a missionary at the Allegheny reserve. Much of what is known about Handsome Lake in these years comes from the Quaker material (Deardorff 93).

Cornplanter called a council to consider Handsome Lake's revelations. They asked the Quaker Simmons what he thought of it, and Simmons responded that sometimes white people fell into trances, in which they saw the good place and the bad place. Simmons said he didn't see why it would be any different for an Indian. That was a remarkable response, because missionaries other than Quakers probably would have seen the visions as visitations of evil. The Quakers desired converts, but did not require a total rejection of tradition, as some other missionaries required (Deardorff 92).

Cornplanter opposed some of Handsome Lake's ideas. The prophet thought that children should not be educated, except for some designated to understand the white man's ways, but otherwise he was opposed to school learning, apparently thinking it might have negative effects. Cornplanter thought that education was important, and the Quakers had established a nearby school. Cornplanter also opposed Handsome Lake's strong dislike of witches. The result of these conflicts was a split in the community, resulting in a new settlement not far away, a village at a place called Cold Spring, which followed Handsome Lake's teachings (Deardorff 96).

Handsome Lake had described to Simmons how the white people had killed their own savior, Jesus. Simmons retorted that it was the Jews who killed Jesus, and that the Indians might be descended from the Jews. The idea that the Indian peoples were descended from the lost tribes of Israel was common at the time. Simmons was amazed at the remark and wondered where Handsome Lake got his information about Jesus from (Deardorff 92).

The prophet's earliest message condemned alcohol, abortion, witchcraft and charms. The Messengers elaborated and told Handsome Lake that the Creator was opposed to adultery, wife beating, the abandonment of children, abandonment of wives, the neglect of children and the elderly and a mother-in-law's interference in a marriage. Handsome Lake preached that the people should give up the longhouse as a residence and build single family homes and give up hunting and fishing to take up agriculture (Encyclopedia "Handsome").

Some of the messages concerned the social ravages of widespread alcoholism. It had led to violence in families, and Handsome Lake's focus on men treating their wives and children kindly and without violence is a direct result of that social trauma. It was also related to spending money on alcohol rather than family needs. Alcohol induced violence also regularly had resulted in killings. The code placed a strong emphasis on the family, on men and women treating each other with kindness and respect, and on good treatment of children.

Before the prophet's visions, the Allegheny Seneca and others would once or twice a year gather up what they had to trade, including furs, deer hams, bear skins, tallow, and other items, and go on a trading visit to Pittsburgh, then the closest city. Merchants there would provide alcohol, expected by the visiting Indians, and much of the proceeds from what they had to sell would be used to purchase alcohol. The return of the traders resulted in extended periods of drunkenness and what was described as violence and debauchery, sometimes resulting in death (Deardorf 93).

After the prophet's teaching took hold, these semiannual trading visits literally became more sober and the money from selling their products went more for tools, food, clothing and items the families really needed. Merchants in Pittsburgh had previously sweetened the trade with alcohol but switched to water (Deardorf 93).

Handsome Lake was opposed to cruelty to animals and described how white people sometimes mistreated their livestock. He was ambivalent about education, thinking it was corrosive of tradition, but that some youth should be educated so as to better deal with the white people in legal and political matters. He warned about private ownership of property and encouraged cooperative farming.

Handsome Lake differed from other Native American prophets in how he regarded white Americans; rather than prophesying that they would be swept away or would simply vanish, he taught that the people could live among them, albeit as a separate community. Overall, Handsome Lake was neither assimilationist nor nativist, but sought to reinvigorate Seneca life by combining some traditions and useful ways adopted from the whites (Encyclopedia "Handsome").

His message was clearly influenced by Christianity, although to what extent is controversial. His message bridges the traditional Iroquois way of life, with its cultural base of hunting and gardening, with a small population over a large area, and the reality emerging around 1800 (Tucker 196).

The prophet was violently opposed to witchcraft. Not long before his visions, a witch suspected of causing the death of a niece of Handsome Lake and Cornplanter had been killed by being stabbed to death by one of Cornplanter's supporters (Izzo 114).

Perhaps the least admirable aspect of Handsome Lake's ministry is that he was associated in 1809 with the execution of several people thought to be witches. It's not clear how he was involved in these ritual murders. He may, in fact, have ordered the executions, or it may have been the act of zealous supporters. The killings of these witches aroused a furor among the Iroquois and resulted in an angry dispute with Cornplanter and threw his teachings into some disrepute. His influence was considerably damaged by the episode, whatever his actual participation may have been. He essentially stopped preaching about witchcraft and was never again involved in the persecution of witches (New World "Seneca").

A mid-20th century recreation of Handsome Lake's recital was done by Ray Fadden, a Seneca, in 1955. Fadden and some assistants created a large beadwork in wampum style, which portrayed the various visions. He combined this with some of the traditional recital to retell aspects of Handsome Lake's experience for his students.

According to Fadden, Handsome Lake told his people that they should shorten the morning period for a deceased family member or friend. He said that sadness in this world made the dead person's spirit sad, and since it took ten days for the spirit to reach the next world, the mourning period should last only ten days, and end with a feast with a place set for the deceased, who would know and be glad (Fadden 352).

Fadden elaborated on the Sky Journey vision in which Handsome Lake was guided along the spirit road (apparently the Milky Way). He was shown an angry white man with a gun, who was jabbing a bayonet into the earth. The messengers told him that the white men were fighting Indians in the west and wanted the Iroquois to help them kill the western Indians, but that the Iroquois must refuse. On the spirit road, they saw George Washington, who had been known in real life as "The Burner" because he had ordered the expedition during the Revolution that destroyed Iroquois power. He was the only white man living there because while he had ordered the expedition that burned out the Seneca, he had allowed the Seneca to remain on their lands and not forced to leave for the west (Fadden 353).

The Messengers led Handsome Lake to a fork in the spirit road. The left fork was wide and promised easy travel. The fork on the right was narrow and rough. The messengers took him a little way down the wide road, and he saw the huge iron house of the Evil One, and he saw the horrible punishment of sinners. Then the messengers took him a short way down the right fork, where he saw a happy land full of forests, with a plentitude of fruit, berries and nuts, and he heard birds singing. He saw his recently deceased niece and his dead son, walking arm-in-arm, followed by other deceased family, all alive in the good land. And he saw his dog who had also died, who recognized Handsome Lake and ran to him, which told Handsome Lake that animal spirits also go to the spirit world (Fadden 354-55).

Ray Fadden's shortened version agrees closely with other accounts of the prophet's experiences with the three messengers and the trip on the Sky Road. The Good Message remains viable and an important link among the various Seneca and Iroquois groups.

The emphasis Fadden placed on Handsome Lake's reform of mourning customs is important. Traditional mourning for the dead lasted for a year and placed many restrictions on the mourners. Confining mourning to ten days resulted in lessening the burden of mourning in a time of lessening population and resources.

In 1800, Handsome Lake was elected to the Seneca tribal council. Among the things they debated, was the sale of land along the Niagara River. He strongly opposed the sale, because in his visions, the Creator had told him that the people must hold on to their land. The land was sold despite his objections. New York's population was exploding, and the land probably would have been taken from them, anyway.

The Iroquois council also sent some of the members to visit Thomas Jefferson in Washington, to discuss matters of land and relationship with the federal government. It is not clear whether Handsome Lake and Jefferson had conversations with each other, although Jefferson would have been fascinated by an Indian prophet. Jefferson's famous letter to Handsome Lake stemmed from this visit.

Handsome Lake's vision and preaching was rather widely known, and President Thomas Jefferson probably learned something about it during the visit. Jefferson wrote a lengthy letter to Handsome Lake in November of 1802, something that impressed the Iroquois and contributed hugely to the prophet's credibility. Some converts interpreted the letter as the federal government formally recognizing Handsome Lake's message, and that the letter meant Jefferson's specific endorsement (Jefferson Papers).

Jefferson began the letter "Brother Handsome Lake," and continued, "I am happy to lean that you have been so favored by the divine spirit as to be made sensible of those things which are for your good and that of your people." Jefferson was referencing the prophet's strong stand against alcohol, which was a notoriously devastating factor in Indian life at the time, one Jefferson was concerned about (Jefferson papers).

The lengthy letter detailed alcohol's baneful impact, describing alcohol's impact on Indians, "It has weakened their bodies, enervated their minds, exposed them to hunger, cold, nakedness and poverty." Jefferson went on to say that the problem was the intemperate and improper use of alcohol that was the problem, not alcohol itself.

Jefferson's letter then turned to the matter of land. Settlers wanted Indian land in New York, and federal agents were trying to work out how to retain some land for Indian needs and yet open land up for settlement. The letter said that the sale of land for a fair price was not apt to be injurious - Handsome Lake wanted to retain all the remaining Iroquois lands and may have told Jefferson that.

Jefferson pointed out that because the people no longer relied on hunting and fishing, they no longer needed so much land to support themselves. The argument that small populations of Indians only needed a small amount of land was a common idea among Americans at the time, and Jefferson described how it is advantageous for a people, as well as an individual, who have more land than they can improve. He wrote, "To sell a part, and lay out the money in stock and implements of agriculture for the better improvement of the residue, a little land, well stocked and improved will yield more than a great deal [of land] without stock or improvement" (Jefferson Papers).

The argument he made in the letter was essentially what was the nation's policy for Indians for more than the next century: settle Indians on land, turn them into farmers, and turn over the excess of the reserved lands to settlers to convert into farmsteads. Handsome Lake actually might have agreed that improving the land would sustain the tribe better, but he would not have been convinced to let go of reservation land.

Jefferson's letter ends with a compliment, still mixed with assimilation. "Go on then brother in the great reformation you have undertaken, persuade our red brethren to be sober, and to cultivate their lands; and their women to spin and weave…" The letter ends with "it will be a great glory for you to have been the instrument of so happy a change and your children's children, from generation to generation, will repeat your name with love and gratitude forever" (Jefferson Papers).

Despite the assimilationist tone and recommendations in the letter, the fact that Handsome Lake received a letter from a sitting President of the United States was unique and highly valued. It contributed greatly to the prophet's status, even by Iroquois who did not accept his teachings.

As the War of 1812 approached, the Indian peoples were acutely aware that tensions were building and were aware of the 1811 battle of Tippecanoe in Indiana, in which Indiana Territory Governor Harrison had defeated a movement based on the teachings of the Shawnee Prophet Tenskwatawa. The Iroquois held a council at Onondaga in September of 1812, and then wrote to the President that they saw trouble coming, but that "The good prophet of the Seneca tribe" had told them to remain at peace. Handsome Lake probably attended this council, but it's not certain if he did (Deardorff 96).

Americans did attempt to recruit Indians for the war, and a few joined the American forces. One of the main theaters of the war of 1812 was the Niagara frontier, where New York State and Ontario are separated by the Niagara River that flows north, connecting Lake Erie and Lake Ontario. Both the British and the Americans used Indians as scouts and sometimes as troops. American recruiters seem to have had little luck recruiting in areas where Handsome Lake's influence was felt. The Iroquois were done with war (Deardorff 96).

During his last several years, Handsome Lake experienced both rewards and strife. He had led a faction away from Burnt House, the Cornplanter village settlement and established another village where he was the chief and where the residents followed his preaching. The news of his new religion spread far enough for a band of Shawnee to visit, and request he return with them, which he refused. His nephew, Red Jacket, saw him as uselessly clinging to the old religion. He accused Red Jacket of witchcraft, and Red Jacket accused Handsome Lake of manufacturing his visions. The strife perpetuated personal conflicts (Native Roots).

In 1815, Handsome Lake was asked by the Onondaga to visit them and share his views. He set out to go there, and on arrival was near death, and died there, with the fourth messenger visiting him and saying the Creator was calling him. He was 80, a remarkably old age for anyone of any ancestry at that time.

Handsome Lake's Legacy

None of the Iroquois languages or dialects had any kind of writing. Tradition and history were maintained by annual recitals, aided by memory devices like wampum belts. The oral traditions seem to have been recalled with remarkable accuracy over long periods of time. The Six Nations met in council once each year, and recitals of history, legends and religion were part of the ceremonies that were conducted at the council meetings. The meetings were for both dealing with current situations, socializing and for affirming the Nations' unity. Handsome Lake's Code was transmitted in this tradition.

Among the Six Nations, there was an elaborate kind of constitution called the *Gayanashagowa*, or Great Law of Peace, which was periodically recited at council meetings and seasonal celebrations, using wampum belts as a memory device to help the narration. Handsome Lake's Code would be read the same way, although it was written down some decades later. The speaker would be solemn, dressed appropriately in fine clothes, speak in a formal manner, and use symbols of the Iroquois past and unity.

The Good Message, as the Six Nations called it, did not threaten anyone, so it did not draw the kind of opposition and repression that messages from other prophets like Wovoka and the Ghost Dance did. That may have helped the Six Nations maintain a separate existence and avoid the kind of severe paternalistic supervision that characterized the Lakota reservations. The fact that Iroquois warfare had come to an end after the American Revolution also helped prevent the close supervision the Lakota experienced.

Starting about 1818-20, a variety of evangelical Christians targeted the Seneca and other Iroquois. Many converted, but Handsome Lake's message allowed many to resist conversion and helped to maintain many traditions that the missionaries would not have permitted (Deardorff 97-98).

Settlers, the state and the federal government kept whittling away at Seneca lands. A particularly controversial attempt was the Treaty of Buffalo Creek in 1838. The Seneca who signed the treaty gave up all remaining reservations in New York: Buffalo Creek, Allegheny, Cattaraugus and Tonawanda. The Seneca were manipulated out of these lands but were assisted again by concerned Quakers. In 1842, there was a supplemental treaty added to the Buffalo

Creek Treaty, and eventually three of the small reservations were recovered. In 1858, the Seneca managed to buy back some of the Tonawanda reservation (Martin).

The sale of the reservation lands was part of an effort to get rid of the Seneca and the other Iroquois in New York and move them to Indian Territory. Some of the Seneca were moved, and some of those forced to move died along the way. Today, there is a Seneca-Cayuga Nation in Oklahoma, one of several Seneca groups.

The Six Nations experienced many changes over the generations following the death of Handsome Lake. The Seneca internal politics included a kind of revolution in 1848 that transferred power from the chiefs to a more democratic kind of government. The Seneca Nation split in two, into the Seneca Nation of Indians and the Tonawanda Band of Indians. The teachings of Handsome Lake gradually became a religion over the period 1818-1845 and has come to be informally called the Longhouse Religion (Martin).

The many accounts of the Iroquois were written down in French and English by traders, missionaries and visitors. Handsome Lake's visions and preachings were mentioned by several visitors, most importantly by Quaker missionaries, in English. However, the code was recited in the native languages, and not written down by Indians themselves for many years. It was remembered and recited from memory at various ceremonies. Small differences and discrepancies inevitably crept in, bringing into question which version was truest to Handsome Lake's original message.

Variations that crept into the text concerned some of the Iroquois. In the late 1840s, Handsome Lake's grandson, Jimmy Johnson, was appointed to consider the versions of the code and then recite an authoritative version. He did so at a longhouse council meeting and continued to do so at a number of longhouse meetings through the 1850s, although he himself had converted to Christianity (Britannica "Gawwiio").

A Seneca named Ely Parker listened to Johnson's recitation of the code at Tonawanda. Parker transcribed it and translated it into English in 1845 and made notes on another Johnson recital of the code in 1848. The recital took portions of three days. Parker had a remarkable career, later becoming the secretary and adjutant to general Ulysses S. Grant during the Civil War, becoming a Union general himself, and later the first Indian head of the Bureau of Indian Affairs (Deardorff 99).

Parker's written version was not the only one. In the 1850s, Chief John Jacket, a Seneca from the Cattaraugus band, was chosen to listen to differing versions and decide which was the authoritative interpretation. He wrote it down in the Seneca language, using a script devised by Rev. Asher Wright, a missionary. This version was somehow lost, although it seems to have been memorized by several. The recitals continued to differ (A. Parker 7-8).

At the time of Handsome Lake's visions, there were still believers and practitioners of the ancient Iroquois religion. By the time of the Civil War, those old beliefs had faded and most of the Iroquois belonged either to a variety of Christian groups or were believers in Handsome Lake's Longhouse Religion (A. Parker 13).

What eventually became accepted as the most authoritative version of the Code of Handsome Lake passed orally through Owen Blacksnake, Henry Stevens and Edward Cornplanter. The tradition was passed among these men orally, so variations crept in. In 1913, Edward Cornplanter edited the version recorded by Arthur Parker, and organized it in numerical sections. This version has come to be considered authoritative. Parker was Seneca. The code is written in the form of descriptive stories about what the messengers or the Creator said and showed to Handsome Lake, and each section is designed to be recited out loud at ceremonies over three days. This version has codified Handsome Lake's visions into a kind of orthodox text.

The sections touch on many things. Section 10 says that men and women in a marriage must not hit each other or abuse each other and should show kindness. Section 14 says that children should be talked to in a kindly way, that discipline should be mild and not include hitting, although splashing water in the child's face or ducking a child's head in water may be done if the child persists in disobedience (Cornplanter).

Section 19 specifies helping the elderly. Section 24 says that boasting is evil, using the example of a vain handsome man. Section 39 says the world will end in 300 years (which would be the year 2100). Section 26 says that two youths from each of the six nations should be chosen to be educated, to study and understand white man's ways. Section 30 says that there are four things that will bring the people happiness: the Great Feather Dance, the Harvest Song, Sacred Songs and the Peach Pit game.

Section 92 describes the only white man allowed near Heaven, the first U.S. president, George Washington, because he did not take Indian land away and respected Indian people. Section 94 describes meeting a man, Jesus, although not naming him; Jesus points to his wounds and says the whites did not understand, and the people will be lost if they follow the way of the white man (Cornplanter).

Overall, the code describes how Handsome Lake had visions and what he saw and was told, ways of behavior that will please or displease the Creator, things that the people should do to assure a welcome in the afterlife and avoid the evil place, and how the people should treat each other, marriage and children. People should work hard, share, respect each other, avoid violence and treat nature well. They should respect children and the old and learn to use the best of the white man's ways.

The code is commonly called Gaiwiio (also spelled Gai'wiio' and Gai: wiio') by followers. It is sometimes called the New Religion. It is recited in abbreviated forms at some of the remaining ceremonies, including the Green Corn ceremony, other ceremonies and particularly at the Midwinter ceremony. It is recited in full every other year at the Six Nation's Conference.

Other ceremonies include the Great Feather Dance, drinking strawberry juice, a form of confession. Some of the ceremonies and meetings are held in buildings designated as a "longhouse," although architecturally, it may be far from the original timber and bark structure (Smith).

There are about 125,000 Iroquois today, and the Seneca are still the most numerous of the Six Nations. There are seven small reservations in New York, one in Wisconsin and five reserves in Canada, as reservation lands are called there. Those in New York are on what once were Iroquois lands, although most of the traditional lands were lost before 1800, with considerable loss since then as well. A significant number do not live on the reservations, with sizable communities in Syracuse and Buffalo, and other cities in New York (deMott).

Handsome Lake's Code is still followed by several thousand Iroquois. The Longhouse Religion allows people to belong to other religions, so some Iroquois follow Catholicism or other Christian religions, or may follow no particular religion at all, and still participate. For some, it is a way of life, and for others, it's a cultural activity that affirms their belonging to the Haudenosaunee community.

There is a vigorous community of followers in Canada, on the Kahnawake, Grand River, Oneida and St. Regis reserves (Smith).

The code is lengthy and is recited in abbreviated forms during such celebrations as the Green Corn Ceremony in late August or early September, and the important Midwinter Ceremony in January or February. It's recited in full every other year (Smith).

The Oneida people in Wisconsin still honor Handsome Lake as a prophet and the Code of Handsome Lake, also called the "Good Message," reaffirms tradition and offers guidance still, in the 21st century. Some Oneida there follows his code, and it is still recited during some events as a way of affirming tradition. The tribal web site refers to the four messengers that gave Handsome Lake the Good Message. It also helps maintain a sense both of being Oneida and of kinship with other Haudenosaunee groups (Williams).

The Seneca-Cayuga Nation in Oklahoma descends from Iroquois and Cayuga in Ohio who were forced to relocate to Indian Territory in the 1830s. They were less influenced by Handsome Lake's teaching, but they maintain tradition, and the influence of his code is evident.

Their site describes how a speaker recites traditional Seneca beliefs and offers a detailed description of the Strawberry Festival as it is currently held. The tiny wild strawberries gathered by women are most prized and are considered good medicine. They were given by the Creator to signify caring for the people. Commercial strawberries are pressed into yielding juice, which is ritually drunk as a rite, a little of it poured on the ground as honoring the ancestors (Seneca).

The Onondaga Nation site strongly emphasizes tradition. Children are born into a clan, and clan members are considered kin to a member of the same clan in other Haudenosaunee groups. The clans are wolf, turtle, beaver, snipe, heron, deer, eel, bear and hawk, the same as in Handsome Lake's Day; he was born into the Wolf Clan and adopted into the Turtle Clan.

Members of the Onondagas still celebrate traditions such as the Midwinter festival, the Strawberry ceremony, the Green Corn celebration and others. Celebrations often have designated speakers who recite legends, history and the Good Message. The Onondaga also summon other groups to councils the traditional way. A string of wampum, created to express a specific concern, is sent to the other groups. The meeting date is sent along with the wampum string, using a notched stick. The stick is cut at the notches, one day at a time. These formal touches perpetuate the tribal culture and symbolize the unity of the peoples, even though they have been scattered for two centuries (Onondaga).

The Six Nations conferences are held at the Tonawanda longhouse in New York. Handsome Lake's code is read in full there every other year, with a part read each of several mornings. The recitations are formal, solemn and are regarded as an essential part of the peoples' Six Nations identity (Tooker "Religion" 35-36).

Online Resources

Other books about Native American history by Charles River Editors

Further Reading

Britannica.com. "Gai-wiio." Encyclopedia Britannica. britannica.com/topic/gai-wiio/. Accessed

 January 17, 2022.

Cornplanter, Edward. "Code of Handsome Lake." Edited by Arthur Parker, 1913. Online at

Sacred Texts.com. sacred-texts.com/nam/iro/parker/. Accessed 18, 2022.ed January.

Deardorff, Merle. "The Religion of Handsome Lake, Its origin and Development." *Bureau of American Ethnology Bulletin 149*, 1951. Smithsonian Institution. Repository.si/edu/ handle/10088/22071/. Accessed January 17, 2022.

deMott, D.K. "Iroquoians." Encyclopedia.com. encyclopedia.com/history/united-states-canada/

north-american-indigenous-peoples/Iroquoian. Accessed January 22, 2022.

Encyclopedia.com. "Handsome Lake." May, 2018. Encyclopedia.com/people/philosophy -and-religion/philosophy-biographies-handsome-lake/.Accessed January 16, 2022.

Fadden, Ray. "The Visions of Handsome Lake." *Pennsylvania History 22* (4), October 1955. JSTOR. Accessed January 20, 2022.

Hamalainen, Peka. *Lakota America*, New Haven, CT: Yale University Press 2019.

Izzo, David. "The Shawnee Prophet and Handsome Lake." Open Journal, Carlton University 108-31. ojs.library.carleton.ca/article/download/. Accessed January 24, 2022.

Jefferson, Thomas. "Brother Handsome Lake." *The Papers of Thomas Jefferson*, July 1-12, 1802. Volume 38. Princeton, NJ: Princeton University Press, 2012."

Martin, John. "Saints, Sinners and Reform, the Burned Over District Prophets.*" Crooked Lake Review,* Fall 2005. crookedlakereview.com/books/Saints_Sinners/Martin3.html. Accessed January 24, 2022.

Mohammedi, Sara. "The Interpretation of Christianity by American Indian Prophets." *Indigenous Nations Studies Journal* 3 (2), Fall 2002. 71-88.

National Park Service. "The Clinton-Sullivan Campaign." nps.gov/fost/historyculture/the-western-expedition-against-the-six-nations-1779.htm/. Accessed January 20, 2022.

Native American Roots.net. "Handsome Lake, Founder of the Longhouse Religion." Nativeamericanroots.net/diary/610. Accessed January 20, 2022.

New World Encyclopedia. "Seneca Nation." neworldencyclopedia.org/entry/Seneca-nation/. Accessed January 18, 2022.

Onondaga Nation of New York. "Culture." Onandaganation.com/culture. Accessed January 25, 2022.

Parker, Arthur. "The Code of Handsome Lake, the Seneca Prophet." Education Department Bulletin, November 1, 1912, the New York State Museum.

Richter, Daniel. "War and Cultures: The Iroquois Experience." *William and Mary Quarterly* (40) 4. JSTOR. 528-59. Accessed January 25, 2022.

Seneca-Cayuga Nation of Oklahoma. "About." sctribe.com/. Accessed January 25, 2022.

Smith, Derek. "Handsome Lake Religion." *The Canadian Encyclopedia.*

thecanadianencyclopedia.ca/en/article/handsome-lake-religion/. Accessed January 18, 2022.

St. John, Donald. *The Dream Vision of the Iroquois: Its Religious Meaning*. Dissertation, Fordham University, 1981. Research.library.fordham.edu/dissertations. Accessed January 20, 2022.

St. John, Donald. "Iroquois Religious Traditions." Encyclopedia.com. encyclopedia.com/environment/encyclopedia-almanacs-transcript-and-maps/Iroquois-religious-tradition/. Accessed January 18th, 2022.

Taylor, Alan. *American Revolutions. A Continental History 1750-1804*. New York: W.W. Norton, 2016.

Tooker, Elisabeth. "On the New Religion of Handsome Lake." *Anthropological Quarterly* 41 (4). Accessed JSTOR. October 1968. 187-200.

Tooker, Elisabeth. "On the Development of the Handsome Lake Religion." *Proceedings of the American Philosophic Society* 133 (1), March, 1989. 35-50.

Wallace, Anthony. "Halliday Jackson's Journal to the Seneca Indians 1798-1800." *Pennsylvania History*. 14 (2) April 1952. 117-147. Accessed JSTOR January 20, 2022.

Wallace, Anthony. "Handsome Lake and the Great Revolution in the West." *American Quarterly* 4 (2), summer 1952. 149-65. Accessed JSTOR January 20, 2022.

Wallace, Paul. "People of the Long House." *American Heritage* 6 (2), February 1955. americanheritage.com/people-long-house/. Accessed January 18, 2022.

Wallace, Paul. "The Iroquois. A Brief Outline of Their History." *Pennsylvania History* 23 (1), March 1959. 15-28. Accesed JSTOR, January 20, 2022.

Williams, Lou. Jr. "Handsome Lake and Kaliwihyo." Oneida Nation. oneida-nsn.gov/our-way/our-story/historic-timeline/handsome-lake-and-kaliwhhyo/. Accessed January 17, 2022.

Free Books by Charles River Editors

We have brand new titles available for free most days of the week. To see which of our titles are currently free, click on this link.

Discounted Books by Charles River Editors

We have titles at a discount price of just 99 cents each day. To see which of our titles are currently 99 cents, click on this link.